Nail Salon Success
A Guide to Creating a Thriving Beauty Business

Table of Contents

Chapter 1. Introduction

Welcome to our Special Report: "Nail Salon Success: A Guide to Creating a Thriving Beauty Business!" This vibrant and inspiring guide is your golden ticket into the colorful world of nail salons, exploding with opportunities and chances for success. Our report is brimming with business insights, delightful tips, and success stories from leading nail salon owners who transformed their creative passion into a booming enterprise. If you've ever dreamt of owning a thriving beauty business, or if you're looking to take your current venture to new heights, this Special Report is just the polish you need to shine. Let's delve in, and let your journey to glittering success begin!

Chapter 2. Harnessing Your Passion: Turning Love for Art into Business

Finding an intersection where passion and profitability meet can be a challenging quest. However, as a lover of nail art, you are one step ahead in this journey. We'll start by identifying what you love most about this industry before discussing how to leverage these passions into a bona fide business.

2.1. Art Appreciation: Understanding The Foundations

Start by appreciating your love for nail art. Understanding the origins of your passion can help you build a strong foundation for your business and keep you driven as you navigate the challenges of entrepreneurship. Is it the exquisite artistry of crafting intricate designs on tiny canvases? Is it the opportunity to work with myriad colors and materials? Or perhaps it's the joy of creating something beautiful and seeing it admired by others. This acknowledgment of what fuels your artistic passion is crucial to maintain motivation and align your business values.

2.2. Art Mastery: Cultivating Skills and Creativity

Nail art is a rapidly evolving space, teeming with opportunities for imagination and uniqueness. To stay ahead of the curve, it's vital to continuously refine your skills and ramp up your creativity. Attend workshops, join online courses, read up on trend reports, and practice different techniques. Hands-on experience is priceless in this field - every nail you paint sharpens your skills and broadens your creativity. Keeping this consistency is essential to establishing your artistic mastery and credibility within the industry.

2.3. Business Acuity: Bridging the Gap Between Art and Entrepreneurship

While a passion for nail art might be the heart of your business, business acuity forms the logical brainpower that leads your entity towards success. Understanding business essentials like budget planning, marketing strategies, customer relations, and even business laws is crucial. Consider enrolling in a business course or seeking a mentor in the industry. Hard work, smart decisions, and a lot of patience form the trifecta of entrepreneurship.

Chapter 3. Blending Art and Profitability

Now that you've mastered your art and brushed up on your business skills, it's time to merge them. This process involves detailed planning and strategic decisions, like pinpointing your target market, setting up your nail salon, and pricing your services optimally.

3.1. Finding Your Niche: Attracting Your Ideal Clients

The first part of amalgamating artistry and commerce is identifying your niche or target audience. Do you resonate more with trendy, fashion-forward clients, or does your art style appeal to a more classic, sophisticated crowd? Understanding your style and clients' aesthetic preferences can help narrow down your audience and tailor your marketing efforts accordingly.

3.2. Creating Your Space: Setting Up Your Salon

The next step is bringing your business vision to life. Your nail salon or studio should reflect your brand's essence and vision while providing a comfortable space for your clients. Aesthetics and functionality should walk hand-in-hand. Focus on the layout, lighting, and decor of your salon space. Make sure it invites, inspires, and embodies your artistry.

3.3. Pricing for Profit: How Much Should Your Services Cost

Pricing is a sensitive area that is crucial to your business's profitability. It must reflect the quality of your service, the time and resources used, and the market rates. Underpricing will not sustain your business in the long run, while overpricing might deter potential clients. Do market research, price comparatives and constantly evaluate your pricing strategy.

3.4. Building Your Brand: Standing Out in a Crowded Market

One way of ensuring success is distinguishing yourself in a saturated market. Building a strong brand – through a unique name, logo, and consistent marketing message – can help carve out a distinct business identity. Social media platforms, your own website, and local networking events are excellent ways to showcase your nail artistry and bolster your brand's visibility.

Chapter 4. Nurturing and Growing Your Business

With your business up and running, it's time to focus on nurturing it and fostering growth. This phase typically involves customer relationship management, staying on top of industry trends, and continually improving your craft.

4.1. Consistent Customer Experience: Retaining Your Clientele

Happy customers are repeat customers. Apart from exceptional nail services, pay attention to the overall customer experience in your salon. A stellar interaction from booking to the finishing strokes of polish can make your salon the go-to place for nail services. Make your customers feel valued – offer loyalty programs, listen to their feedback, and ensure your customer service is top-notch.

4.2. Staying Trendy: Updating Your Skills and Services

Keeping your finger on the pulse of the nail industry is crucial for success. Changes happen rapidly – new nail trends emerge, technology evolves, and customer preferences shift. Regularly updating your skills and offering new services will keep your business relevant and competitive. Participate in continuing education, industry events, and online forums to stay informed.

4.3. Expanding Your Horizons: Opportunities for Growth

Even as your business thrives, always look ahead for expansion opportunities. Could you introduce new services, collaborate with other local businesses, or open another location? Entrepreneurship is a constant journey of growth, innovation, and learning. It's not just about how far you've come, but how much further you can go.

Your love for nail art, coupled with a robust business mindset, can help turn your passion into a profitable business. This journey needs dedication, persistence, and constant growth. It won't be easy, but with every nail you paint, every challenge you overcome, you are one step closer to making your passion your livelihood.

Chapter 5. Setting Up Your Studio: Choosing the Right Location

Choosing the right location for your nail salon is of great importance; it determines not only your establishment's visibility but also your ability to attract and retain clients. It's tantamount to the lifeblood of your business, setting the stage for your salon's ambiance, accessibility, and overall success.

5.1. Observing Competitor Locations

Before choosing your nail salon's location, research existing competitive salons in your target area. Visit these salons to understand better their choice of location, types of clientele, proximity to complementary businesses, parking availability, etc. Additionally, paying close attention to their business hours can provide insights into the area's peak operating hours.

Analyze these traits critically:

Location: Are they located in an affluent neighborhood, a business district, or a residential area? **Types of clientele**: Are the customers students, office workers, residents, or tourists? **Proximity to complementary businesses**: Are they near shopping centers, office buildings, or universities? Are there popular cafes or restaurants nearby that attract a lot of foot traffic? **Parking availability**: Is there ample parking close to their salon?

Take detailed notes and use this information as a benchmark when selecting your salon location.

5.2. Assessing Foot Traffic

In the beauty business, visibility is key; the more people that pass by your salon, the higher the chances of attracting walk-in clients. Therefore, it's essential to choose a location with high foot traffic. Areas near shopping centers, restaurants, and office buildings are prime locations as they're usually frequented by potential customers.

To assess foot traffic, visit your desired location at different times and days of the week. This will give you an accurate picture of how many people are passing by the salon location throughout the day.

5.3. Proximity to Complementary Businesses

Consider setting up your nail salon near businesses that complement rather than compete with your services. Businesses like hairdressing salons, beauty supply stores, and clothing boutiques attract a similar clientele and can be beneficial in drawing in potential customers.

Bear in mind that being located near successful businesses implies thriving surroundings and for your salon, it suggests a steady stream of potential customers. On the other hand, pay attention to nearby businesses that may produce unpleasant odors (e.g., restaurants), which could affect your salon's ambiance and customer experience.

5.4. Parking Availability

Although foot traffic is crucial, don't overlook your car-driving clients' needs. Many clients appreciate the convenience of a nearby parking facility. Limited or no accessible parking can discourage clients and impact your business negatively, especially in cities where people prefer to drive.

If a nearby parking facility isn't available, consider partnering with local businesses to use their parking or opt for a location within a short walk from public parking.

5.5. Safety of Location

Ensure that the area you choose for your nail salon is safe and well-lit, especially after sunset. A safe and secure environment will make your clients feel comfortable visiting your salon even during late hours.

5.6. Customer Demographics

Your target customers' demographics play a huge role when choosing your salon location. For instance, if you're planning to provide luxury services, then you should opt for a location in a affluent neighborhood. On the other hand, if your target customers are students, a location near a university would be more appropriate.

Carry out a demographic study of your target area, looking at factors such as age, gender, occupation, income level, and lifestyle preferences. This information will help you understand the area better and ascertain if it's suitable for your target market.

5.7. Accessibility

Is your salon easy to access for both clients and employees? Consider factors like its distance from major roads or highways, availability and reliability of public transport, and ease of direction (i.e., is it easy to find?).

5.8. Lease Considerations

Before you sign a lease, carefully review its terms and conditions. Pay close attention to the length of the lease, rent escalation clauses, who is responsible for repair and maintenance, and any restrictions on business hours or signage.

It's advisable to work with a commercial real estate broker or attorney to help you understand and negotiate better terms.

5.9. Salon Size and Layout

The size of your salon will determine several crucial factors, such as the number of clients you can accommodate at once, the number of nail technicians you can employ, and the types of services you can offer. Consider current as well as future needs.

The layout of the salon is vital as well. You need to have enough space for workstations, a waiting area, a retail section (if you wish to sell products), and storage.

5.10. Legal and Regulatory Considerations

Different localities have varying licenses, permits, and zoning laws for businesses. Research these requirements before settling on a location to avoid legal issues. Visit your local city hall or business regulatory office to get the necessary information or seek advice from a business attorney.

Choosing your salon location might seem a daunting task, but with careful planning and thorough research, you can find a location that will set your business up for success. Weigh the factors discussed here carefully and choose a location that aligns with your business model, target clientele, and budget. A strategic location can do wonders for your nail salon's visibility and profitability, ultimately bringing you closer to achieving your business aspirations.

Chapter 6. Finances 101: Budgeting, Pricing and Profit Maximization

In the realm of beauty business, your financial prowess holds as much weight as your artistic skills. From planning budgets to setting prices and maximizing profits, these factors significantly contribute to your nail salon's success. Through the mastery of finance, you can transform your passion into a thriving and lucrative business.

6.1. Budget Planning and Tracking

The first step toward financial health is to map out a comprehensive budget and regularly track your expenses. Begin with initial expenses, including salon design, equipment, supplies, furniture, and fixtures. Also, consider costs for hiring staff, insurance, licenses, and marketing. These form your startup costs. Next, identify your ongoing costs like rent, utilities, salaries, supplies restocking, and marketing. Your budget should clearly reflect all these aspects.

If you're new to business, consider hiring an accountant or using budget software to ensure accuracy. Record all expenditures, categorize them accordingly, and evaluate them regularly. By doing so, you avoid over-spending and ensure every dollar is used productively.

6.2. Setting Up Prices

The right pricing strategy can make or break your nail salon. To start, analyze your costs, both fixed and variable, to help set your minimum price point. Then, research what competing salons in your area are charging. Visit their websites, make phone calls, or even go as a visitor.

A hefty price tag may lead to lost clients. On the other hand, low pricing could undercut your profits and undermine your brand's perceived value. Seek a balance - a price point that not only covers your costs and ensures profitability but also matches the quality of your service.

Consider different pricing strategies such as tiered pricing based on experience level of the technician, bundled packages for multiple services, or loyalty discounts for regular customers.

6.3. Salary Management

Your staff's payment is another crucial aspect. Remember, in the beauty industry, your technicians' skills directly impact your salon's reputation. Therefore, pay competitively to retain talent. Consider various compensation models like hourly wage, commission-based, or a hybrid model. Also, keep in mind that beyond the basic salary, you are legally obligated to handle taxes, social security, and possible benefits.

6.4. Profit Maximization

Maximizing profit isn't solely about cost-cutting; it also involves increasing operational efficiency and revenue. For efficiency, consider strategies like minimizing waste, better inventory management, and staff scheduling. For revenue, upselling, cross-selling, retailing beauty products, and providing additional services can significantly enhance your sales.

6.5. Regular Financial Assessments

Set aside time each month to review your finances thoroughly. By regularly unpacking your income, expenditures, and profit margins, you can spot trends and make necessary financial decisions quickly. Tiny shifts in your finances can add up over time, impacting your business significantly.

6.6. Dealing with Tax and Legal Obligations

Taxes can be a complex area to navigate. Get acquainted with local, state, and federal taxation for businesses. For this, consider hiring a tax consultant who specializes in small businesses. It's essential to keep business finances separate from personal ones. This simplifies bookkeeping and tax processes and offers some legal protection.

Keep a clear eye on your salon's financial health using these strategies. Your financial aptitude paired with your beauty skills can set your nail salon on a success trajectory you've always dreamt of.

Remember that while handling finances may seem daunting at first, it's integral to your business. Business acumen is just as vital as creativity in building a thriving nail salon. As you grow, so will your knowledge and confidence in managing these critical aspects. This financial comprehension will ensure you not only survive but thrive in the beauty industry, turning your dream into a sparkling reality.

Chapter 7. Standing Out: Curating Unique Service Offerings

In the bustling world of nail salons, creating a unique service offering is the key to distinguishing yourself from the myriad of competitors vying for your clientele's attention. By curating a distinctive blend of services, you can appeal to a wider and more diverse audience while cultivating a unique brand identity that resonates and endures.

7.1. Defining Your Specialty

Your specialty is the core of your unique service offering. By identifying what you do best, you can leverage this skill to attract clients and establish your salon as the go-to destination for this particular service. In defining your specialty, it's essential to take into consideration your skills, interests, and the demand in your market.

Here is a potential workflow:

1. List all the services you and your staff can perform.
2. Identify the services you are most proficient at and enjoy delivering.
3. Research market demand to verify the viability of these specialty services.
4. Decide on your specialty based on your findings.

Creating a niche doesn't mean you have to exclude other services. Rather, it enables you to focus your marketing efforts on what sets you apart. It serves as your unique selling proposition (USP).

7.2. Surveying the Market

Understanding your market is an integral step. This includes identifying your potential clients, their preferences, and the competition. Here's a simple way to perform a market survey:

1. Identify the demographic you want to serve.

2. Conduct interviews, online surveys or focus group discussions to gauge their wants and needs.

3. Scout local competition to note their strengths and weaknesses.

4. Utilize this data to carve a niche for your salon.

This research not only informs your unique service offerings but also aids in crafting a persuasive marketing strategy.

7.3. Value-Adding Services

Distinctive and value-added services could be the deciding factor for a customer when choosing a salon. These are some suggested value-adding services:

1. Nail Art Design Consultation: Offering consultation services, where professionals advise clients on the best nail art designs that suit their style or event theme.

2. Mobile Nail Services: Providing in-home services for clients who value convenience and personalization.

3. Nail Health Workshops: Offering workshops focusing on nail health and home care tips.

4. Subscription Packages: Designing comprehensive packages for clients who frequently utilize your services.

7.4. Collaborative Partnerships

Collaboration with local businesses can be an effective strategy to enhance your service offering. For example, partnering with a local café could result in a 'manicure and brunch' package. A collaboration with a yoga center may result in a 'wellness package' that includes a yoga class and a manicure. These partnerships could make your salon stand out and increase your customer base.

7.5. Customer Experience

Superior customer experience should be the cornerstone of your service offerings. Fast and efficient service, inviting salon ambiance, professional and friendly staff – all these factors contribute to an unforgettable customer experience. The significance of cleanliness and sanitary practices cannot be overstated, especially in the post-pandemic era.

7.6. Continuing Education

To stay ahead, make it a priority to stay updated on industry trends and technological advancements. Attending industry expos, enrolling in online courses or certifications, and networking with other industry professionals could keep you on top of changes and provide an edge.

7.7. Regularly Revise Your Service Menu

Your service offerings should not be set in stone. As trends and client needs evolve, so should your offerings. Regularly revisiting your service menu allows you to phase out less popular services and introduce new, exciting ones.

By shaping and refining your unique services, you can stand out from the crowd, attract and retain a loyal customer base, and achieve sustainable business growth. While this endeavor requires strategic planning, systematic implementation, and ongoing optimization, the resulting success is certainly worth the effort. Therefore, starting to curate your unique service offerings today is a giant leap towards securing your place in the competitive beauty industry of tomorrow.

Chapter 8. Knockout Techniques: Essential Nail Art and Care Skills

Understanding and mastering the realm of nail care and art is the foundation of any successful nail salon. Packed with professional secrets, innovative techniques, and tried-and-true methodologies, this chapter gives you an in-depth look at the beauty skills you need to turn an ordinary salon visit into an extraordinary one.

8.1. Essential Tools of the Trade

When it comes to nail care, having the right tools in your arsenal is essential.

1. **Nail Files and Buffers:** Choose various grit levels that suit different stages of nail filing. A 240-grit file is perfect for shaping, while a 600-grit buffer lends a glossy finish.

2. **Cuticle Nippers:** Essential for nail prep, they remove dry skin and hangnails for a clean nail bed.

3. **Manicure Bowls:** These cater to soaking hands and softening cuticles before treatments.

4. **Nail Clippers:** A salon-grade nail clipper is essential for achieving the perfect length and shape.

5. **Nail Brushes:** They're used to clean the nails and the surrounding skin.

6. **Nail Polish, Gels, and Lacquers:** A good selection of quality products is unquestionable.

An organized workspace enhances your efficiency and service experience for the client. Try compartmentalized drawers or toolbelt to store your stationary items nearby.

8.2. Knowing Your Client's Hand Anatomy

A successful nail technician knows that understanding their client's hand anatomy is the key. Factors like the nail's arch shape, lunula visibility, or even the client's skin oiliness can affect the final result of a manicure.

Always assess the client's hands, nails, and their lifestyle before beginning any process. It helps tailor the service to their needs and ensure the durability and longevity of the manicure.

8.3. Nail Hygiene and Sanitation

Workplace hygiene is paramount. It builds trust with clients and ensures their safety. Always sanitize your tools before and after each use. Use a salon-grade disinfectant for tools and surfaces, and sterilize your tools after every client. Disposable items, like nail files and buffers, must be replaced after every use.

8.4. Art of Nail Shaping

Nail shaping can entirely change how hands look. Master different shapes, including:

1. **Square:** This shape is great for wide nail beds.

2. **Oval:** Suitable for small hands and short fingers.

3. **Almond:** For slender fingers and narrow nail beds.

4. **Squoval:** Universal, working well with most finger and nail types.

Practice your skills and understand how each nail shape complements the overall hand aesthetics.

8.5. Mastering Manicures and Pedicures

These are fundamental services your salon needs to excel. It's not just about polish application, but also exfoliating, moisturizing, and massaging. A great manicure or pedicure feels like a spa experience. Offer variations, such as traditional, spa, or gel, and unique experiences like hot stone pedicure or paraffin dip.

8.6. Gaining Proficiency in Polish Application

Polish application is a skill every nail technician must perfect. Whether it's a glossy lacquer, durable gel, or a long-lasting dip powder, your ability to apply it seamlessly determines the outcome of your service.

Creating crisp and clean lines around the cuticles, applying polish in thin even layers, and ensuring the polish does not flood the cuticles are important aspects. Always remember to seal the free edge to prolong the manicure's life.

8.7. Trendy Nail Art Techniques

Nail art is huge in the beauty industry, and staying ahead of trends is necessary. Be it intricate designs, abstract art, or minimalist touches, offer a varied menu to cater to every client's unique taste.

1. **Stamping:** Create intricate designs with ease using specially designed stamps and plates.

2. **Sponging:** Ideal for creating ombre effect or galaxy designs.

3. **Water Marbling:** A unique technique resulting in complex psychedelic designs.

4. **Hand Painting:** This is the most basic, but it requires immense skill to master.

5. **Rhinestones and Decorations:** Add luxury and glamour to any manicure by using jewels, sequins, or foil.

Workshops and online courses are a great way to learn and keep up with changing trends.

8.8. Creating a Comfortable Atmosphere

Beauty services are as much about the experience as they are about the result. Develop an inviting atmosphere by considering ambient music, subtle scents, comfortable chairs, and refreshing drinks. A memorable salon visit gives you loyal clientele and increases your referrals.

In conclusion, nailing these techniques elevates you from a nail technician to a "nail artist", allowing you to create beautiful experiences around your services and cultivate a loyal clientele. Keep honing your skills, stay updated with the changing trends, and remember, every hand you touch is a canvas waiting for your artistic touch. Your journey towards a successful nail salon is ready for takeoff.

Chapter 9. Mastering Customer Relationships: Service, Satisfaction, and Retention

Long-standing relationships with customers are the lifeblood of any business, especially the beauty industry. In a world where beauty salons are ubiquitous, excellent customer service leading to customer satisfaction and retention becomes a major distinguishing factor. Businesses that can not only draw in new clients but also retain them are the ones that thrive.

9.1. Knowing your clients

In a service-oriented industry, the first step to building strong customer relationships is understanding your clientele. Analyzing demographic data like age, gender, occupation, and income levels can be immensely helpful. However, the core of knowing your clients lies in understanding their individual preferences, lifestyle, beauty needs, and expectations of your services as well as the experience at your salon.

Getting feedback from customers regularly and staying open to their suggestions is crucial. If possible, implement feedback systems like suggestion boxes or online surveys that lets your clients express their opinions freely. This will prove invaluable in improving your service quality and adjusting your offerings to meet the real-time demands of your clients, hence establishing an empathetic relationship.

9.2. Consistency in service quality

Once you've got to know your clients, it's vital to maintain consistently high service quality. There is no 'one-size-fits-all' approach here - what works for one client might not work for another. Keep your staff up-to-date with ever-changing beauty trends and train them continuously to ensure they deliver expert, personalized services.

Customer satisfaction is directly proportional to the quality of service you provide. If people leave your salon feeling pampered, they are more likely to return.

9.3. Building staff-client relationships

People tend to do business with people they like; similarly, clients will prefer coming back to the same nail technician if they form a positive rapport. Therefore, building strong staff-client relationships can be a great strategy for customer retention.

Ensure that your team is trained in soft skills alongside their technical expertise. Being courteous, attentive, and patient are as important as being skilled in the art of manicure/pedicure.

Reminding your clients about the value your team brings in and fostering a culture where clients get to know their technicians on a personal level can do wonders in building trust and loyalty.

9.4. Reward loyalty

Loyalty schemes can be instrumental in customer retention. Offering loyalty cards that provide discounts or free services after a certain number of visits, or offering exclusive deals and early-bird discounts to regular clients, are just a few ideas to get started here.

9.5. Customer recovery

While satisfying every customer is the goal, you should also have a well-defined strategy for customer recovery. There may be instances when a client is dissatisfied with the service. How you respond in such situations can define your relationship with that customer henceforth.

Always listen to your clients' complaints or critiques without defensiveness. Apologize sincerely and seek to remedy the situation as best you can. Offering compensation like a refund or free service can demonstrate your commitment to customer satisfaction, even in unfortunate situations.

9.6. Use of technology

In an era of fast-paced technology, your customers also expect savvy solutions from you. Implementing an online booking and payment system, sending confirmation and reminder messages on mobile devices, offering digital catalogs of various styles, are some of the ways to enhance the customer experience and drive customer satisfaction and retention.

In conclusion, these strategies, when implemented right, can turn your salon from just a beauty service provider into a community beloved by its clients. Mastering the art of customer service, satisfaction, and retention is undoubtedly a lengthy process, but the rewards are plentiful.

Your clients are not just patrons – they are your partners, brand ambassadors, and the very core of your business. Investing time, training, and resources in building healthy, lasting relationships with them will yield exponential returns. Don't just aim to meet expectations – strive to exceed them. It's the key to creating a thriving beauty business that will shine with success.

Chapter 10. Nitty Gritty of Marketing: Advertising and Promoting Your Salon

The success of a nail salon lies not merely within the skills of its nail techs or the quality of its services, but in its ability to market those services effectively. With the fierce competition in today's beauty industry, knowing how to advertise and promote your salon is crucial to staying ahead.

10.1. Understanding Your Market

Your first step towards marketing your salon is to understand your market. This involves identifying who your target customers are and understanding their needs, preferences, and purchasing habits. Gathering this information can be accomplished through market research, which can involve surveys, focus groups, or studying industry reports and statistics.

Remember, your target audience is not simply 'everyone.' Different customer groups have different needs and preferences when it comes to nail care services. By understanding who your 'ideal' customer is, you can tailor your services and advertising efforts to match their needs and tastes.

10.2. Building a Strong Brand

Establishing a recognizable brand for your salon is a vital part of your marketing strategy. A brand goes beyond just a logo or a tagline - it is what people associate with your salon, its services and staff, and it influences how consumers perceive your business.

When building your salon's brand, consider what makes your salon unique. Is it your focus on eco-friendly practices? The luxurious and relaxing experience you offer? Or perhaps it's a particular type of nail art that you specialize in? Whatever it is, make sure that this USP (unique selling point) is communicated clearly and consistently through your branding.

10.3. Crafting an Effective Advertising Strategy

Advertising comes in many forms, from traditional avenues such as newspaper ads, TV commercials, and billboards to modern digital advertising channels like social media, email newsletters, and Google Ads.

While the form of advertising you choose depends largely on your budget and target audience, a balanced mix of both traditional and digital advertising will likely bear the most fruit. Don't forget that word-of-mouth – or its modern equivalent, online reviews – can be a powerful and cost-effective form of advertising too.

Traditional newspapers and local magazines can help reach an older demographic, while digital advertising is more effective for a younger, tech-savvy audience. Social media ads, in particular, are a popular and effective choice for nail salons because of their ability to reach a broad audience and their targeting options that allow you to reach potential clients based on their interests and demographics.

10.4. Promotional Activities and Special Events

Promotions and special events are excellent ways to attract new customers and retain existing ones. Offering discounts, special packages, or freebies can incentivize potential customers to try your services, while hosting events like nail art workshops or ladies' nights can foster a sense of community around your salon.

Consider turning holidays or special days (like Valentine's Day, Mother's Day, Christmas, or even National Nail Polish Day) into promotional opportunities. Spa parties are another great idea; these can be birthday parties, bridal shower parties, or simply friends getting together to pamper themselves. You can extend your services to corporate companies too, for events like corporate wellness or team building.

10.5. Establishing your Online Presence

In this digital age, having a strong online presence is essential. This can be in the form of a professional website highlighting your services, prices, and contact details, or an active social media profile showcasing your work and client testimonials, or ideally, both.

Social media platforms like Instagram are particularly useful for nail salons, as they allow you to showcase your work visually. Regularly posting pictures of your nail art, behind-the-scenes glimpses of your salon, and special promotions can keep your salon top-of-mind for your followers when they need a nail treatment.

Don't neglect online reviews either. Encourage your happy customers to leave a review on your Google My Business profile or other review websites. These online testimonials can significantly impact potential customers' decisions to choose your salon.

10.6. Building Relationships through Excellent Customer Service

Excellent customer service cannot be overstated in its importance. It can turn a first-time client into a loyal customer and lead to great word-of-mouth referrals. Ensure that your staff are trained not just in their nail tech skills, but also in interpersonal skills.

Remember, although you're in the nail salon business, you're also in the 'people business.' Creating a welcoming, friendly environment will encourage clients to return. This includes knowing your regular customers' preferences, offering a comfortable and clean salon environment, and showing genuine appreciation for your clients.

To recap, effective marketing for your nail salon involves understanding your target market, building a strong brand, crafting an effective advertising strategy, offering promotions and events, establishing a strong online presence, and building relationships through excellent customer service. By following these steps diligently, your salon will not only attract new customers but also retain existing ones, leading to a thriving nail salon business.

Chapter 11. Becoming the Go-to Salon: Building Your Brand and Reputation

The cornerstone of a thriving nail salon is its brand. A carefully curated, visually pleasing, and easily recognizable brand is key to attracting and retaining customers. Just as you meticulously create beautiful designs on nails, your brand must be designed with the same attention to detail. It forms the first impression potential clients have before they even set foot in your salon, so it's crucial to get it right.

11.1. Building a Strong Brand

A strong brand tells customers what to expect. It can elicit emotions, rouse curiosity, and create a sense of excitement about visiting your salon.

1. **Define Your Brand**: Start by understanding who you are and what your salon represents. What are your core values? What unique services or experiences can you offer that set you apart from other salons? Maybe you use only cruelty-free products, or you have expert nail artists who can create any design a customer brings in. Your brand should reflect these aspects.

2. **Identify Your Target Audience**: Think about the type of clientele you want to attract. Are you catering to a luxurious, high-end market, or aiming to create a warm, friendly environment for everyday people? Your branding should align with this identity.

3. **Create a Unique Visual Identity**: Your logo, color palette, style, and even the fonts you use form your salon's visual identity. Make sure it's consistent across all platforms, from your storefront sign and business cards to your website and social

media pages.

4. **Communicate Your Brand Consistently**: Once you've established your brand, communicate it consistently. Every touchpoint a potential or current customer has with your salon should reinforce your brand's message.

11.2. Enhancing Salon Atmosphere: An Integral Part of Your Brand

The atmosphere created in your salon is a tangible representation of your brand and it plays a huge part in defining customer experience. Are you a plush, relaxing retreat, or a bright and happy place that buzzes with energy? Whichever it may be, create an environment that makes your clientele want to return.

1. **Décor and Design**: Decorate your salon keeping your brand identity in mind. The smallest details like the wall colors, chairs, lighting, and even the music can make a significant difference.

2. **Cleanliness and Hygiene**: A clean and sanitary environment is non-negotiable. Any compromise here not only tarnishes your brand but poses health risks.

3. **Customer Service**: Train your team to provide exceptional service. This includes greeting customers warmly, listening to their needs and preferences, and providing relevant suggestions.

11.3. Building a Stellar Reputation

A strong brand supported by an inviting atmosphere will set the stage for success, but a stellar reputation will confirm your status as the go-to salon.

1. **Deliver High Quality**: Delivering consistent service quality is paramount. Ensure your nail technicians are skilled, trained

regularly, and aware of the latest trends and techniques.

2. **Address Issues Promptly**: Address any customer issues promptly and professionally. Standing by your services and righting any wrongs will earn you credibility.

3. **Request Reviews**: Encourage happy customers to leave positive reviews online. Positive reviews can lead to more footfall, while responses to bad reviews (if any) demonstrate your commitment to customer satisfaction.

4. **Commit to Professionalism**: Make professionalism a cornerstone of all business activities. Be prompt in appointments, respect your clients' time, uphold strict staff attire and behavior rules, and manage business finances diligently.

11.4. Social Media: A Powerful Tool to Elevate Your Brand

In today's digital era, social media platforms offer a wide platform for showcasing your brand and building your reputation.

1. **Actively Use Social Media**: Regularly post before-and-after photos, videos of nail art processes, or posts highlighting your unique services or products. Not only does this showcase your work, but it also keeps your brand fresh in customers' minds.

2. **Engage with Your Audience**: Answer queries promptly and show your appreciation for positive comments. This connection builds a community around your brand.

3. **User-Generated Content**: Encourage customers to share photos of their nails after a visit to your salon with a specific hashtag, helping you reach a wider audience.

4. **Influencer Partnerships**: Partner with local influencers. Their posts can help you reach a larger audience and add credibility to your salon's reputation.

Building your nail salon into the go-to place requires careful planning and execution to create a strong brand, maintain a consistent, inviting atmosphere, uphold stellar service quality, and use social media effectively. A combination of these elements will build your salon's reputation and make you shine in the nail salon industry. It's a journey filled with creativity and hard work but, ultimately, it's a journey towards a thriving beauty business.

Chapter 12. Proven Success Strategies: Learn From Renowned Salon Professionals

To mention industry titans without talking about their strategic approach would be like skipping basecoat when applying nail polish – the end result just wouldn't hold. Thus, we unveil the strategies that lead to their lasting success.

12.1. Adopt a Customer-First Approach

Building a successful nail salon goes beyond offering top-tier services and products. It requires continuously nurturing relationships with your customers, always putting their needs at the very heart of your operations.

Cheryl Greenfield, owner of the award-winning Greenfield Nails & Spa in Arizona, stands as a testament to this approach. Cheryl notes, "In our line of work, it's really about ensuring that customers are satisfied above and beyond their expectations. We continually train our staff to listen to our customers, understand their needs and desires, and provide that extra level of personal touch."

12.2. Diversify Your Service Offering

In an increasingly competitive marketplace, offering a diverse range of services is key. Veronica Vargas, owner of V Nails in Chicago, emphasizes the importance of diversification in her success. "When we added unique services like dip powder nails and 3D nail art, we saw a significant spike in our bookings," she explains. "Staying abreast of the latest trends and incorporating them into your service line-up is paramount to stay relevant and attract a broad clientele."

12.3. Invest in Quality Staff Training and Retention

Employees are the backbone of any successful nail salon; they are the ones delivering the customer experience. Theresa Clifford, who runs glossy Tip Top Nails in LA, swears by her policy of investing in staff training. "We make sure our team is skilled in the latest techniques. It's an investment that has always paid off through happier, more loyal clients, and our uniquely high retention rates."

12.4. Elevate Your Salon's Ambiance

The ambiance of your salon plays a significant role in attracting and retaining customers. Gemma Clarke, who skyrocketed her salon, Gem Nails, in New York from start-up to a well-known name, says, "Customers don't just come for a manicure or pedicure; they come for the nurturing environment. We've always aimed to create that welcoming, retreat-like atmosphere, where clients feel pampered."

12.5. Leverage the Power of Technology

The right technology can streamline your salon's operations, boost efficiency, and elevate the client experience. Emma Bryan, owning a chain of successful nail salicants, E-Nails, speaks on the transformative power of technology. "Booking appointments changed for us when we started using salon management software. It not only freed up our receptionist's time but also provided a more convenient booking process for clients. Utilizing social media to showcase our work attracted new customers, too."

12.6. Build Strong Partnerships

Creating industry relationships is a strategic move for increasing your salon's reach and reputation. Sarah Hong, the mind behind The Nail Lab in San Francisco, has experienced the benefits first-hand. "I've benefitted greatly from partnering with high-quality suppliers, fellow beauty salons for cross-promotions, and even local businesses for special packages. These partnerships brought in new clients, and helped to cement our brand's reputation."

12.7. Stay Conscious of Health and Safety

Top salon operators prioritize the health and safety of their customers and staff. This is echoed by Beverly Hills-based salon owner, Laura McAllister, who attributes part of her success to her salon's strict adherence to health and hygiene protocols. Laura says, "A clean, safe salon not only ensures client and staff well-being, but also builds trust and loyalty."

12.8. Value Feedback and Continuous Improvement

Lastly, successful salon operators understand that there's always room for growth and improvements. James Reynolds, owner of three thriving salon locations under JR Nails banner, explains, "We conduct regular customer feedback surveys and staff meetings to identify areas for improvement. It's a strategy that's led to continuous improvement and has helped us stay ahead."

Ultimately, carving out your unique path in the nail salon industry involves a healthy blend of these strategies. But remember, the most robust business models are those that remain adaptable and open to change. Now, with the proven success strategies of established salon professionals within reach, you're well on your way to painting your own success story.

Chapter 13. Future-Proof Your Business: Trends, Innovation, and Growth Strategies

Change is the only constant in our world, and the beauty industry is no exception. To secure a profitable future for your nail salon business, one needs to be in tune with the trends, unafraid of innovation, and possess a robust growth strategy.

13.1. Understanding Current Trends

Keeping an eye on current trends in the nail beauty industry is a prerequisite for future-proofing your business. Trends can encompass everything from new nail design techniques, emerging nail art styles, to preferred nail shapes and colors by consumers.

One way to stay updated on trends is by following established nail design artists and influencers on social media platforms like Instagram, Pinterest, or TikTok. Moreover, subscribing to trade magazines and attending beauty conventions can also provide insights into popular trends.

The trends are not only relevant to designs but also to products. Consumers are increasingly looking for health-conscious beauty choices, such as non-toxic and vegan-friendly nail products.

13.2. Embracing Innovation

Innovation is the key to success in any business. When it comes to nail salon businesses, innovation could mean anything from offering unique nail art designs to integrating technology into the business model.

1. **Utilising Advanced Technology:** Consider incorporating technology in scheduling appointments, billing, and customer relationship management. There are numerous software applications convenient for these tasks, providing additional convenience for both the business and customers.

2. **Creating Unique Customer Experiences:** Harness virtual reality (VR) or augmented reality (AR) technologies to allow customers to "try on" different nail designs digitally before making a decision.

3. **Offering Cutting-edge Services:** Be the first in your area to provide new techniques and treatments. For instance, nail extensions, Gel and Dip powders, or Organic manicures are currently on the rise.

Remember, innovation should extend beyond technology. Creative marketing strategies, unique customer rewards programs, or partnerships with local businesses can all bring fresh new dimensions to your nail salon business.

13.3. Drafting Growth Strategies

One of the aims of future-proofing your venture is to ensure continuous growth. For this, you must have a solid growth strategy in place. Here are some ideas:

1. **Branching Out:** If your current location is successful, consider opening more salons in areas with similar demographics.

2. **Expand Your Services:** Offering complementary services such as hand massages, waxing, or foot care can increase your average customer value.

3. **Target New Markets:** If your clientele is primarily made up of younger women, consider marketing services for men and older

women.

4. **Invest in Training:** The more skills your staff possess, the broader the range of services you can offer. Regular training sessions with the latest techniques can keep your team fresh and motivated.

5. **Upgrading Your Salon:** Redesigning the interior or upgrading your equipment can make your salon more inviting. Moreover, using premium tools can enhance the overall customer experience.

13.4. Partnering For Success

Future-proofing your nail salon business can be an overwhelming task to do alone. Therefore, considering partnerships is a promising approach:

1. **Product Companies:** Forming partnerships with nail product companies could provide benefits such as bulk pricing, early access to new products, or collaborative marketing efforts.

2. **Local Businesses:** Partnering with local businesses can create mutually beneficial relationships. For instance, offering discounts to employees from surrounding businesses can increase your customer base and boost community relationships.

3. **Influencers and Bloggers:** Collaborating with local influencers or bloggers can raise your salon's profile and get you in front of a wider audience.

Altogether, the future-proofing process and growth strategy for your nail salon business hinge on understanding and leveraging industry trends, embracing innovation, proper planning, and creating beneficial partnerships. Combining these strategies positions your business not just to survive, but thrive in the future, creating a vibrant nail salon that customers love coming back to again and again. Be ready to adapt and innovate, and success will undoubtedly follow your path.

www.ingramcontent.com/pod-product-compliance
Lightning Source LLC
Chambersburg PA
CBHW062304290526
45794CB00006B/2695